SUNDAY BEST QUILTS

12 Must-Make Quilts You'll Love Forever

Sherri L. McConnell and Corey Yoder

Martingale®
Create with Confidence

Sunday Best Quilts
12 Must-Make Quilts You'll Love Forever
© 2019 by Sherri L. McConnell and Corey Yoder

Martingale®
19021 120th Ave. NE, Ste. 102
Bothell, WA 98011-9511 USA
ShopMartingale.com

Printed in China
24 23 22 21 20 19   8 7 6 5 4 3 2 1

Library of Congress Cataloging-in-Publication Data is available upon request.

ISBN: 978-1-68356-004-3

MISSION STATEMENT

We empower makers who use fabric and yarn to make life more enjoyable.

CREDITS

**PUBLISHER AND
CHIEF VISIONARY OFFICER**
Jennifer Erbe Keltner

CONTENT DIRECTOR
Karen Costello Soltys

DESIGN MANAGER
Adrienne Smitke

MANAGING EDITOR
Tina Cook

PRODUCTION MANAGER
Regina Girard

TECHNICAL EDITOR
Ellen Pahl

PHOTOGRAPHER
Brent Kane

COPY EDITOR
Jennifer Hornsby

ILLUSTRATOR
Sandy Loi

SPECIAL THANKS
*Photography for this book was taken at
the home of Tracie Fish of Bothell, Washington.
Instagram: @fishtailcottage*

Contents

Introduction

One of the great parts of life is anticipating what's to come. All of us have things we're looking forward to right now. Whether it's a baby on the way, a new path in life, or something as simple as a weekend away, anticipation is the spice of life. The same holds true for quilters—we savor thoughts of projects to make, fabric to stash, and time to spend in our sewing rooms.

As we began planning this book, we started talking about our "bucket list" quilts, those quilts we've had on our to-do list for years, the ones that would be so special they'd feel like we were bringing out our Sunday best. All quilters have these lists: the "I must make this sooner rather than later" list, the "I need to purchase more fabric for this quilt first" list, and the "I need to dust up my sewing skills for this quilt" list. Whatever the case, we all have quilts we look forward to creating at some point.

We quickly realized that this book was the perfect opportunity to cross off some of the items on our quilty bucket list, and we hope to help you cross some off your list too. After we each came up with our top must-make quilts, we compared ideas and focused on the six favorite quilts we each wanted to make. Our quilt themes are Favorite Star, Scrappy, Red-and-White, Christmas, Pineapple, and Courthouse Steps.

Then came the fun part: we each designed a quilt to fit every theme. We didn't compare notes as we designed, and it's been fascinating to discover the differences in the quilts. We wanted this book to feel a bit like reading through the design journal of a friend, so you'll find interesting tidbits and useful comments, and you'll get to peek into our design process and thoughts as we designed each quilt. You'll find Corey's comments highlighted with coral and Sherri's with aqua.

We hope you love reading through *Sunday Best Quilts* and enjoy making quilted treasures to last a lifetime.

~ Corey & Sherri

Let's Chitchat about That

A book of quilts beloved enough to achieve "Sunday best" status wouldn't be complete without a Sunday best memory or two!

When I was growing up, my family went to church both Sunday morning and Sunday evening. The Sunday evening services were particularly memorable because much of my extended family attended the same church. After the service, especially in the summer, we would all head over to my great-grandparents' house for sweet tea and snacks. Of course, this meant playing all evening with my cousins and sneaking back indoors for an extra cookie. My great-grandparents lived on a farm, so there was always something fun to do, and we played outside until it was too dark to see.

~ Corey

Let's Chitchat about That

I think my favorite Sunday best memory is of when I was six or seven years old. My mom had sewn a gorgeous Easter dress for me, made out of lavender dotted swiss fabric. She loved dotted swiss in every color, but I think lavender was her favorite. I remember her working on the dress and her excitement over making it for me. I got new white shoes, lacy white socks, gloves, and an Easter hat to go with it! A treasured old photograph shows me on the sidewalk in front of our home wearing my Easter finest. Maybe this experience is what led me to sew many dresses while I was in high school and eventually to create my own wedding dress.

~ Sherri

Cultivating a Friendship

We're both quilt designers who also design fabrics for Moda Fabrics. While those things we have in common make a good basis for a friendship, like everyone else, it takes some time to learn about one another and really cultivate that friendship. We live far apart (Corey lives in Ohio and Sherri lives in Nevada), but we get to catch up in person about every six months at Quilt Market. We thought it would be fun to do a little interview with one another so you could get to know us better too.

COREY: Sherri and I first became friends online through our quilting blogs and the online quilting industry. I wish I could remember the first time I chatted with Sherri via email, but it feels as if I've always known her. We met in person at International Quilt Market in the spring of 2015, when we were both showing our first lines of fabric for Moda Fabrics. That was such a fun experience to share. I don't think either one of us knew the other would be showing a fabric line until shortly before Quilt Market. I remember thinking, "Hmmm . . . I wonder if Sherri has ever considered designing a fabric line?" And then having our first lines release at the same time was really neat.

SHERRI: As Corey mentioned, she and I first became friends online through our blogs and the amazing online quilting community. I can't remember when I started following her blog, but it's been one of my favorites! Corey has always created designs I love, and I was super-excited to find out she was going to design fabric for Moda. My daughter and co-designer, Chelsi, and I were able to debut our first collection at the same market as Corey, which was a fun coincidence. Corey ended up being even nicer in real life than I imagined from reading her blog.

How did you become involved in quilting?

COREY: This question makes me laugh when I think back on it. I remember walking into a fabric store shortly after getting married. Now, I had been in lots of fabric stores growing up because my mom was an avid seamstress and quilter. But this particular time I fell in love with fabric: the smells, the colors, and all the textures. I went home that day with fabric purchases. I really hadn't sewn while growing up; I hadn't been interested in sewing. After that fabric bug bit, I began dragging my husband into quilt shops on our vacations and purchasing more fabrics. I knew I needed to figure out something to do with the fabrics I

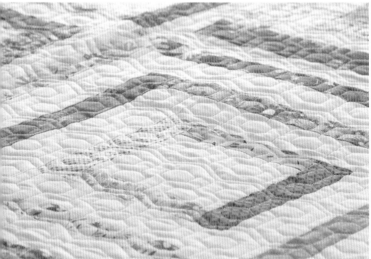

*I fell in love with fabric:
the smells, the colors,
and all the textures.*

-COREY

was accumulating. Quilts were a natural choice because I'd been surrounded by them my entire life. When I stumbled upon the online world of bright, cheerful quilts, less traditional than I was used to seeing, I was hooked.

SHERRI: First, I never thought I'd be a quilter. I sewed clothes for myself, formal wear for others, and clothes for my children. Quilting was something my grandmother did, and I thought she was just a little bit crazy to cut up fabric and sew it back together. But my grandmother wisely helped me make a quilt for my oldest child when he was eight years old, and that was all it took.

Shortly after I began quilting, we moved away from town to a more rural area. I was no longer able to go to quilt guild meetings with my grandmother. Luckily for me, the world of online quilt blogs was just beginning, and I quickly became an avid reader of every blog I could find. Of course, this caused me to start quilting even more!

What made you decide to design fabric?

COREY: Oh, I love this story too. It was the spring before my youngest daughter was going to start kindergarten. I had been a stay-at-home mom up to this point. I was talking to a group of friends, several of whom also had youngest kids starting kindergarten in the fall, and all were stay-at-home moms. We were talking about our plans for the upcoming fall. I had always thought I would head back to work outside the home when both kids were in school. I had a job offer managing a local quilt shop, which sounded like a lot of fun. But as the time approached, I wasn't sure how that would work during the summer or school holidays.

My husband and I waited eight years after getting married to have children, for a couple of reasons. We were very young—I was 19 and he had just turned 23 the week of our

wedding. The second reason was that I wanted to be able to stay home with our kids when that time rolled around. It was still important to me to be at home when they needed me.

I mentioned to my group of friends that I had been thinking a little bit about fabric design. I was laying out the pros and cons of fabric design versus the managerial position, and one of my friends said, "Well you should just do fabric design!" I went home that evening determined to see what I could do to make that happen. About two months after that, I submitted a fabric collection to Moda Fabrics and was welcomed into the Moda family.

SHERRI: Designing fabric always seemed to be a dream job, one I might have had in another lifetime if I had studied graphic design instead of English in college. One Sunday while driving home from an enjoyable quilting retreat, which I had attended as both a teacher and participant, I just could not get the idea out of my head. Suddenly I knew who I had to talk to—my daughter Chelsi, who was that child who drew constantly as she was growing up. I gave her paper and pens and pencils at every birthday and Christmas to try and keep her from drawing on the walls. I knew that if she would agree to work with me, we could design fabric together. Thankfully, she was interested in my idea!

Do you feel there is a color that should be included in every quilt?

COREY: Gray all the way! I love what gray adds to a quilt.

SHERRI: Blue, of course! Blue is definitely my favorite color, but I really love all colors and the way they work together to make the world a beautiful place. Yellow is another favorite color, but it has to be just the right shade.

Quilting was something my grandmother did, and I thought she was just a little bit crazy to cut up fabric and sew it back together.

- SHERRI

Do you have a favorite quilt you've designed?

COREY: The very first quilt I "made" was a Maple Leaf quilt. I say "made" in quotes because in reality, I cut out all the pieces for the quilt and then I sent everything over to my mom, who pieced and quilted it for me. This was when I was still in my buying-fabric-but-not-sewing stage of life. I have always loved Maple Leaf quilts, and a couple years ago I designed a super-scrappy one I call Maple Charm. It really brought my quilting journey around full circle.

SHERRI: My Mahalo quilt has to be my favorite because I based it on a quilt pieced by my great-great-grandmother in the 1930s. My grandmother gave me the quilt, which was in very poor condition. I knew immediately that I wanted to make my own version of it. With the help of modern tools, my quilt was much easier to put together than the original was, I'm sure. I love knowing that I made the same pattern that my ancestor made so many years before!

11

I love to sew with friends and enjoy conversations and the wit and humor of others, but with my busy schedule, that only seems to happen when I get to attend a retreat.

— SHERRI

If you were a quilt block, what block would you be?

COREY: I think I'm going to have to say a Nine Patch block. It's a simple, practical block. It works well with other blocks in lots of different settings. It's not the flashiest of blocks, but it's very versatile.

SHERRI: At first I was going to say a Star block because I love all Star blocks! But really, I've come to love curved piecing, and think I would be a Drunkard's Path block. Life has so many curves that we are forced to deal with around every corner . . . and the Drunkard's Path block shows us that things that don't look like they can fit together really can work! I love the lesson in that.

Do you have a favorite fabric line?

COREY: Right now my favorite line is Sunnyside Up. I really enjoyed working with the fabrics and have designed so many quilts for this line. Sundrops and Pepper & Flax are right up there too.

SHERRI: So far, our Clover Hollow collection has been my favorite. To date, I've pieced eight quilts and several small projects and accessories with it. I'm still having fun with all the combinations and prints and have more projects on the list with this grouping.

How many hours a week do you spend sewing?

COREY: This varies a lot for me. I try to be careful about not spending too much time sewing while my family is at home, which means I spend more time sewing during the school year and try to limit sewing time during the summer and evenings. If I'm away from my machine for too long, though, I start to get a little bit antsy to get back at it!

*If I'm away from my machine
for too long, I start to get a little
bit antsy to get back at it!*
-COREY

SHERRI: My sewing time really varies too. Some weeks I sew for 25 to 30 hours, while other weeks I'm lucky to sew for 10. When my kids were young and still at home, I sewed a lot at night while my husband was away at the fire station. Now I love sewing during the sunny parts of the day and rarely sew late at night.

What do you listen to or watch while you are sewing?

COREY: I enjoy listening to podcasts while I sew. My husband got me hooked on them several years ago. He'd been listening to them since before they were cool. He purchased a little portable speaker for me that allowed me to listen over the noise of my sewing machine. I've been listening ever since. Podcasts are just as bingeable as streaming TV shows!

SHERRI: It's hard to have the television on while I sew because I feel like I miss too much, but I've recently started listening to business and motivational podcasts while sewing. Sometimes I like just having a little quiet. I love to sew with friends and enjoy conversations and the wit and humor of others, but with my busy schedule, that only seems to happen when I get to attend a retreat.

What kind of sewing machine(s) do you have?

COREY: The only machine I had for the first 15 years of sewing was a Bernina Activa 135. I have since added a Juki TL 2010Q as my primary piecing machine. This Juki is a straight-stitch-only machine and it is a delight to piece with.

SHERRI: I have had a Janome Memory Craft 6600 Professional for several years now. Before that I had a Janome Memory Craft 4000, and before that I had a Singer that my mom gave me for our wedding. I travel with a Janome Gem Platinum, which is great; it's lightweight and fits in a carry-on! I also have a vintage Singer that I should really use once in a while.

What time of day are you most productive?

COREY: Definitely mornings . . . my husband wakes me up at 5:30 a.m. when he leaves for work, and I can get so much done with that early start. I'm especially *not* productive, sewing-wise, after about 5:00 p.m.

SHERRI: If I'm up early, I'm super-productive in the morning. Lately I've been trying to time-block, grouping like tasks together; that seems to work well regardless of the time of day.

ON A WHIM

Designed and pieced by **SHERRI McCONNELL**; quilted by **MARION BOTT**

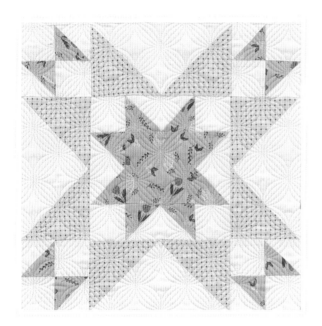

MATERIALS

Yardage is based on 42"-wide fabric. Fat eighths are 9" × 21".

18 fat eighths of assorted prints for blocks and sashing squares
1⅞ yards of cream tone on tone for blocks and inner border
⅓ yard of cream floral for sashing
⅝ yard of navy floral for outer border
½ yard of green print for binding
3⅛ yards of fabric for backing
55" × 55" piece of batting

Star blocks have always been among my favorites, so of course this book had to include a favorite Star block quilt. I especially love making blocks that create secondary patterns even when set together with sashing. The floral sashing reminds me of a trellis, making this a whimsical garden of stars.

Before You Cut

Before cutting, sort the 18 fat eighths into nine pairs so you'll know which will work well together as pairs for the blocks. Also decide which prints you'll use for the inner and outer portions of each block. I laid out my fat eighths and took a photograph with my phone to make sure I liked the placement before I began sewing.

~ *Sherri*

15

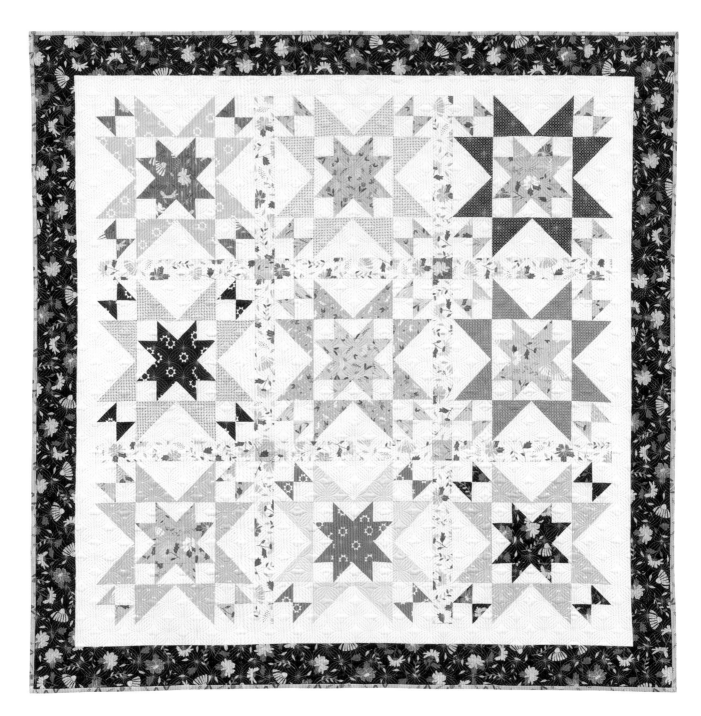

Finished quilt: 48½" × 48½"   ◆   Finished block: 12" × 12"

CUTTING

All measurements include ¼"-wide seam allowances.

From *each of 9* fat eighths (for center stars and corner units), cut:
4 squares, 2½" × 2½" (36 total)
1 square, 3½" × 3½" (9 total)
8 squares, 2" × 2" (72 total)

From *each of 9* fat eighths (for large star points), cut:
8 squares, 3½" × 3½" (72 total)

From the scraps of fat eighths, cut:
4 squares, 2" × 2"

From the cream tone on tone, cut:
6 strips, 2" × 42"; crosscut into 108 squares, 2" × 2"
3 strips, 2½" × 42"; crosscut into 36 squares, 2½" × 2½"
8 strips, 3½" × 42"; crosscut into:
    36 rectangles, 2" × 3½"
    36 rectangles, 3½" × 6½"
5 strips, 2" × 42"; crosscut *2 of the strips* into 2 strips, 2" × 39½"

From the cream floral, cut:
4 strips, 2" × 42"; crosscut into 12 rectangles, 2" × 12½"

From the navy floral, cut:
5 strips, 3½" × 42"

From the green print, cut:
6 strips, 2¼" × 42"

CONSTRUCTING THE BLOCKS

Press the seam allowances as indicated by the arrows in the illustrations. The instructions are written for making one block at a time. For each block you will need the following pieces:

- 4 cream 2½" squares
- 12 cream 2" squares
- 4 cream 2" × 3½" rectangles
- 4 cream 3½" × 6½" rectangles
- A matching set of:
  4 print 2½" squares
  8 print 2" squares
  1 print 3½" square
- 8 print 3½" squares

1. Draw a diagonal line from corner to corner on the wrong side of each cream 2½" square. Place a marked cream square right sides together with a print 2½" square. Sew ¼" on each side of the drawn line. Cut on the drawn line to make two half-square-triangle units from each pair of squares. Trim the units to measure 2" square. Make eight half-square-triangle units.

Make 8 units.

2. Sew two half-square-triangle units and two cream 2" squares together as shown to make a corner unit. Make four corner units that measure 3½" square, including seam allowances.

Make 4 units, 3½" × 3½".

3. Draw a diagonal line from corner to corner on the wrong side of the eight print 2" squares. Place a marked square right sides together on one end of a cream 2" × 3½" rectangle. Sew on the drawn line and press. Trim the seam allowance to ¼". Repeat on the opposite end to make a flying-geese unit that measures 2" × 3½". Make four units.

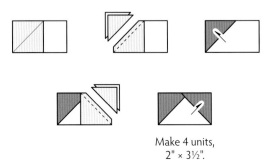

Make 4 units,
2" × 3½".

4. Repeat step 3 with the contrasting print 3½" squares and the cream 3½" × 6½" rectangles. Make four flying-geese units.

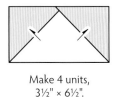

Make 4 units,
3½" × 6½".

5. Arrange and sew four cream 2" squares, four small flying-geese units, and the matching print 3½" square in three rows as shown. Sew the rows together to make the center star, which measures 6½" square, including seam allowances.

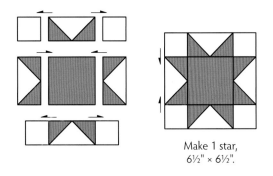

Make 1 star,
6½" × 6½".

6. Arrange and sew the corner units from step 2, the center star, and the four large flying-geese units together in rows. Sew the rows together to make the Star block. The block should measure 12½" square, including seam allowances. Make nine blocks.

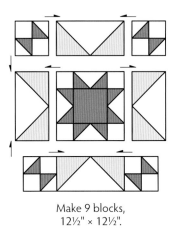

Make 9 blocks,
12½" × 12½".

ASSEMBLING THE QUILT TOP

1. Arrange the blocks in three rows of three blocks each. Move the blocks around as needed to have a good mix of colors and prints throughout the quilt top.

2. Sew the blocks together in rows with a cream floral 2" × 12½" sashing strip between the blocks. Make three rows that measure 12½" × 39½".

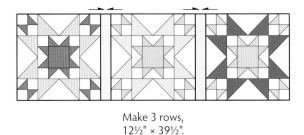

Make 3 rows,
12½" × 39½".

3. Sew three cream floral 2" × 12½" sashing strips and two print 2" squares together to make a sashing row that measures 2" × 39½". Make two rows.

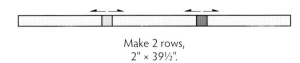

Make 2 rows,
2" × 39½".

4. Join the block rows and the sashing rows as shown in the quilt assembly diagram below. Press the seam allowances toward the sashing rows. The quilt center should measure 39½" square, including seam allowances.

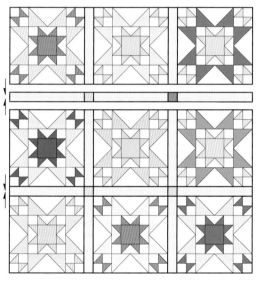

Quilt assembly

5. Add the cream 2" × 39½" strips to the left and right sides of the quilt center. Sew the remaining cream strips together and cut two strips 42½" long. Sew these to the top and bottom. Press the seam allowances toward the border. The quilt center should measure 42½" square, including seam allowances.

6. Sew the navy floral 3½" × 42" strips together to make one long strip. Cut two strips 42½" long and sew them to the left and right sides of the quilt center. Cut two strips 48½" long and sew them to the top and bottom. Press the seam allowances toward the border. The quilt top should measure 48½" square.

FINISHING THE QUILT

For help with any of the finishing steps, go to ShopMartingale.com/HowtoQuilt.

1. Layer the backing, batting, and quilt top. Baste the layers together and quilt as desired. Sherri's quilt is machine quilted in an allover orange-peel variation called Orange Leaf Dark. The curves of the quilting contrast nicely with the angles and straight lines of the piecing and soften the edges.

2. Trim the excess batting and backing. Use the green 2¼"-wide strips to prepare binding and attach it to the quilt.

Let's Chitchat about That

I always like Sherri & Chelsi's fabrics for Moda. They create some of the best low-volume prints to my eye, and a lot of their fabrics mix beautifully with mine. I also appreciate that this quilt will come together quickly. This is one I'm going to need to make sooner rather than later.

~ *Corey*

STARLING

Designed and pieced by **COREY YODER**; quilted by **KAYLENE PARRY**

MATERIALS

Yardage is based on 42"-wide fabric. Fat quarters are 18" × 21".

20 assorted print fat quarters for blocks
5 yards of white solid for blocks
⅝ yard of black stripe for binding
4⅝ yards of fabric for backing
67" × 82" piece of batting

About the Fabric

For this quilt I used Moda's Ombré Confetti Metallic by Vanessa Christenson of V and Co. I had wanted to try the fabrics for a while. Each ombré fabric contains many different shades of one color along the width. Because of this, it looks as if you've cut pieces from more fabrics than you've actually used. I always think a good quilt is one that looks like you spent a lot of time on it, especially if you didn't.

~ Corey

When I am teaching, one of my favorite bits of advice to students is, "It only needs to be as perfect as you need it to be." In other words, don't worry about what others think about your piecing. If you're happy with your blocks and quilt, you are good to go. This quilt is a little bit fussy to piece, but the results are worth it!

Finished quilt: 60½" × 75½" ◈ Finished block: 15" × 15"

CUTTING

All measurements include ¼"-wide seam allowances. Refer to the cutting guide below before cutting the fat quarters.

From *each* fat quarter, cut:
12 squares, 3" × 3" (240 total)
4 squares, 5½" × 5½" (80 total)

From the white solid, cut:
30 strips, 1¾" × 42"; crosscut into 640 squares, 1¾" × 1¾"
37 strips, 3" × 42"; crosscut into 480 squares, 3" × 3"

From the black stripe, cut:
7 strips, 2¼" × 42"

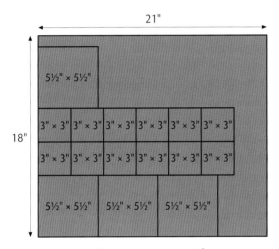

Fat-quarter cutting guide

CONSTRUCTING THE BLOCKS

The instructions are written to make one block at a time. For each block, choose the pieces cut from *one* of the fat quarters. Press the seam allowances as indicated by the arrows in the illustrations.

1. Draw a diagonal line from corner to corner on the wrong side of 32 white 1¾" squares.

2. Place a marked square right sides together on one corner of a print 3" square, orienting the diagonal line as shown above right. Sew on the drawn line. Trim the corner, leaving a ¼" seam allowance. Repeat on each corner to make a square-in-a-square unit that measures 3" square. Make eight units.

Make 8 units,
3" × 3".

3. Draw a diagonal line from corner to corner on the wrong side of 16 white 3" squares. Repeat step 2 using the print 5½" squares to make four square-in-a-square units that measure 5½" square.

Make 4 units,
5½" × 5½".

4. Sew together four 3" square-in-a-square units as shown. The completed unit should measure 5½" square, including seam allowances.

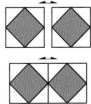

Make 1 unit,
5½" × 5½".

5. Sew together two white 3" squares, one print 3" square, and one 3" square-in-a-square

unit to make a block corner that measures 5½" square, including seam allowances. Make four block corners.

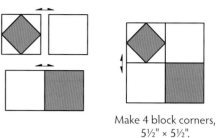

Make 4 block corners,
5½" × 5½".

6. Arrange and sew the units made in steps 3–5 in three rows as shown. Sew the rows together to complete a block that measures 15½" square, including seam allowances. Make 20 blocks, one from each of the fat quarters.

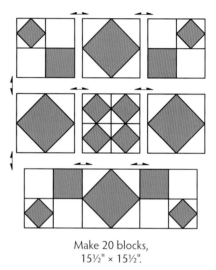

Make 20 blocks,
15½" × 15½".

Pin for Precision

For the most part, I'm not a pinner, but I did pin when piecing these blocks and recommend that you pin too, even if you don't usually. You will especially want to pay attention to how the square-in-a-square units come together. With careful sewing and pinning, you can avoid losing any points and keep your blocks nice and tidy.

~ Corey

ASSEMBLING THE QUILT TOP

1. Arrange the blocks in five rows of four blocks each as shown in the quilt assembly diagram below.

2. Join the blocks in each row and press. Join the rows and press. The quilt top should measure 60½" × 75½".

FINISHING THE QUILT

For help with any of the finishing steps, go to ShopMartingale.com/HowtoQuilt.

1. Layer the backing, batting, and quilt top. Baste the layers together and quilt as desired. Corey's quilt is machine quilted with allover echoing squares.

2. Trim the excess batting and backing. Use the black stripe 2¼"-wide strips to prepare binding and attach it to the quilt.

Let's Chitchat about That

Starling is a dynamic quilt where color seems to be the star, but really, the crisp white stars created by the squares of color are just stunning. I love the secondary patterns in this quilt as well as the terrific color placement.

~ Sherri

Quilt assembly

SWEET CONFETTI

Designed and pieced by **COREY YODER**; quilted by **KAYLENE PARRY**

I'm scrappy at heart—scrappy quilts, that is! One can never have too many scrappy quilts, and goodness knows the scraps are readily available. My favorite scrappy bits are the small ones, too small to use but too pretty to part with. I often choose a mix of sherbet colors when going scrappy, as I love the warm, golden colors of summer.

MATERIALS

Yardage is based on 42"-wide fabric.

96 rectangles, 5" × 10", of assorted prints for blocks
3⅛ yards of white solid for blocks
⅝ yard of diagonal stripe for binding
3½ yards of fabric for backing
61" × 79" piece of batting

CUTTING

All measurements include ¼"-wide seam allowances.

From *each* print rectangle, cut:
1 square, 3⅞" × 3⅞"; cut in half diagonally to make 2 triangles (192 total)
1 square, 4¼" × 4¼"; cut into quarters diagonally to make 4 triangles (384 total; 96 are extra)

From the white solid, cut:
14 strips, 5⅜" × 42"; crosscut into 96 squares, 5⅜" × 5⅜". Cut in half diagonally to make 192 triangles.
6 strips, 4¼" × 42"; crosscut into 48 squares, 4¼" × 4¼". Cut into quarters diagonally to make 192 triangles.

From the stripe, cut:
7 strips, 2¼" × 42"

Finished quilt: 54½" × 72½" ◆ Finished block: 9" × 9"

CONSTRUCTING THE BLOCKS

For each rectangular half-block, you will need a matching set of three small print triangles and two larger triangles. You will also need two small white and two large white triangles. Press the seam allowances as indicated by the arrows in the illustrations.

1. Sew a small print triangle to each small white triangle and press. Sew the units together to make an hourglass unit that measures 3½" square, including seam allowances.

Make 1 unit,
3½" × 3½".

2. Sew a large print triangle to each white side of the hourglass unit as shown.

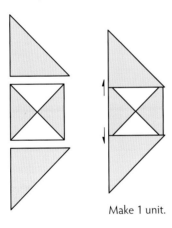

Make 1 unit.

3. Sew a small print triangle to the right side of the unit as shown and press.

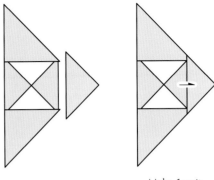

Make 1 unit.

4. Sew a large white triangle to each short side of the unit to complete the half-block. It should measure 5" × 9½", including seam allowances. Make 96 half-blocks, one from each different print.

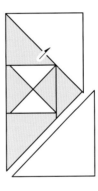 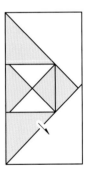

Make 96 half-blocks,
5" × 9½".

5. Sew the half-blocks together in pairs to make a total of 48 blocks that measure 9½" square, including seam allowances.

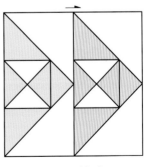

Make 48 blocks,
9½" × 9½".

Let's Chitchat about That

I make hourglass units by making half-square-triangle units first, and then nesting the seams and stitching. (I have a tutorial on my blog.) When making half-square-triangle units (or other corner units), I often save the "waste" triangles to use in other projects.

   This is such a playful design for a scrap quilt—it's sweet and happy! I feel that Corey and I have similar ideas about scrap quilts—both of our projects have simple-to-piece blocks that can be made with a variety of fabrics and then combined into one cheerful quilt. This quilt would be fun to make with leftover triangles from a variety of fabrics!

~ *Sherri*

ASSEMBLING THE QUILT TOP

1. Arrange the blocks in eight rows of six blocks each, rotating the blocks as illustrated in the quilt assembly diagram at right.

2. Join the blocks in each row and press. Join the rows and press. The quilt top should now measure 54½" × 72½".

FINISHING THE QUILT

For help with any of the finishing steps, go to ShopMartingale.com/HowtoQuilt.

1. Layer the backing, batting, and quilt top. Baste the layers together and quilt as desired. Corey's quilt is machine quilted in an allover orange-peel design.

2. Trim the excess batting and backing. Use the striped 2¼"-wide strips to prepare binding and attach it to the quilt.

Quilt assembly

Scrap Advice

If you are ever intimidated by choosing fabrics for a scrap quilt, here are some techniques to help you conquer your nervousness.

◆ If you have a fabric in your stash that you especially love, use it as a jumping-off point for choosing colors for your scrappy quilt.

◆ Choose multiple lines from one designer. Both Sherri and I, as well as many other designers, make sure our lines can be mixed and matched. This takes all the guesswork out of scrappy quilts.

◆ Start with a line of fabric and then add coordinating fabrics.

◆ Choose your palette from a favorite photograph.

◆ Have fun and don't overthink it!

◆ One thing I used to do a lot when I began making and designing my own quilts was to do "fabric pulls" from my stash. These were random, unrelated fabrics that I chose using the list of suggestions above. I would arrange the fabrics together and take a picture of them. This helped me learn how to combine fabrics successfully.

◆ First, you can see how the stash fabrics in your grouping play together. Those big, splashy florals don't tend to work as well in piecing, nor do those novelty prints you are so drawn to. Hmmm . . . this leads to the question of whether you have enough

basics in your stash. They might not draw your eye in the quilt store, but basics are needed in every quilt—solids, near solids (such as Grunge by Moda Fabrics), and tone-on-tone fabrics. Additionally, linen is a fun choice for adding texture to a quilt.

◆ Arranging fabrics together also helps you know which combinations you are really drawn to and what palette you like to work with. You may be able to see which prints from different designers work nicely together. Also pay attention to the "genre" of fabrics you have in your stash. That oddball Civil War reproduction fabric you have tucked away isn't going to play as nicely with those modern geometric prints.

◆ You will quickly see that a quilt needs a balance of fabrics to make it successful. A variety of larger florals, smaller florals, basics, and smaller geometrics is essential when pulling fabrics. Playing with the fabrics in your stash will give you experience with how fabrics work together before you even begin cutting.

◆ Lastly, snap a picture. A photo captures colors and prints in a way your eyes can't see on their own. What you think is a medium value may turn out to be a dark or a light. This trick will help you fine-tune your fabric choices in any project.

~ Corey

DRIFTWOOD DRIVE

Designed and pieced by **SHERRI McCONNELL**; quilted by **MARION BOTT**

MATERIALS

Yardage is based on 42"-wide fabric.

64 assorted light squares, 5" × 5",
    for blocks
1 Moda Jelly Roll *or* 40 strips, 2½" × 42",
    for blocks
¼ yard *total* of assorted prints for blocks
⅝ yard of fabric for binding*
4 yards of fabric for backing
71" × 71" piece of batting

Sherri made a scrappy binding using 21" strips of assorted prints. For a similar binding, you'll need 14 strips, 2¼" × 21".

There's something irresistible about a scrap quilt. I have favorites with hundreds of different fabrics and others with just dozens. Either way, I like to piece scrap quilts with a simple design so the fabrics can become the star. The simple block in this quilt fits the bill and provides an introduction to partial-seam construction.

About the Fabrics

I've always loved the combination of blues and yellows and was happy to find a fun collection of them in the Harmony Group by Sweetwater. I mixed in some other Sweetwater fabrics plus some of Corey's Pepper & Flax. These soothing fabrics and the simple block design make for some wonderfully homey scrappy goodness!

~ Sherri

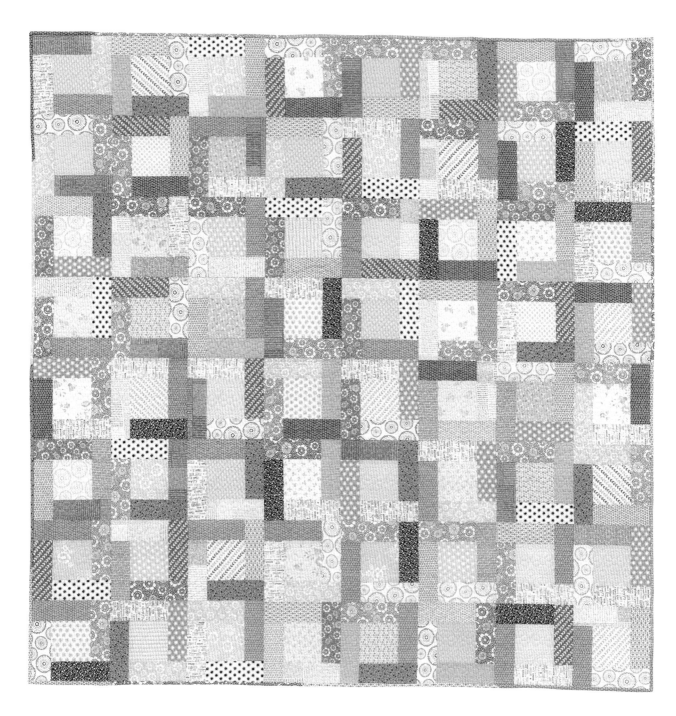

Finished quilt: 64½" × 64½"   Finished block: 8" × 8"

34

CUTTING

All measurements include ¼"-wide seam allowances.

From the 5" × 5" squares, cut:
64 squares, 4½" × 4½"

From *each* of the Moda Jelly Roll strips, cut:
6 rectangles, 2½" × 6½" (240 total)

From the assorted prints, cut:
16 rectangles, 2½" × 6½"

From the binding fabric, cut:
7 strips, 2¼" × 42"*

*For the scrappy alternative, cut 14 assorted strips, 2¼" × 21".

Choosing Fabrics

For ease in fabric selection and cutting, you can simply use a charm pack, a Moda Jelly Roll, and a fat quarter of coordinating fabric (rather than scraps). But it's fun to raid your scrap bin. Extra Moda Jelly Roll strips and Layer Cake squares (10" × 10") will also work for cutting out many of the block pieces. Additionally, the binding can be pieced from extra Jelly Roll strips. If you use two Jelly Rolls and a charm pack, you can omit the quarter yard of assorted prints and you'll have enough for the quilt top *and* binding.

~ Sherri

CONSTRUCTING THE BLOCKS

Press the seam allowances as indicated by the arrows in the illustrations.

1. For each block, choose one 4½" square for the block center and four 2½" × 6½" rectangles for the sides.

2. Place the 4½" center square right sides together with a 2½" × 6½" rectangle as shown. Sew a 3" seam beginning at the edge of the square, leaving part of the rectangle unsewn.

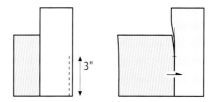

3. Rotate the unit and sew a 2½" × 6½" rectangle to the adjacent side. Press.

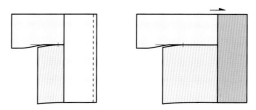

4. Sew a third 2½" × 6½" rectangle to the unit and press.

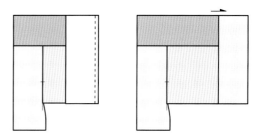

5. Fold the loose end of the first rectangle out of the way and add the fourth 2½" × 6½" rectangle. Press.

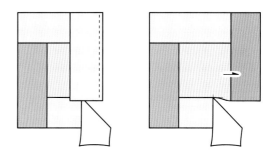

6. Finish the block by sewing the remainder of the partial seam. Press. The block should measure 8½" square, including seam allowances. Make 64 blocks.

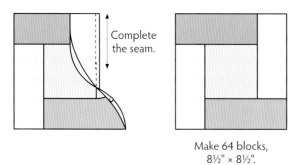

Make 64 blocks,
8½" × 8½".

Complete
the seam.

Let's Chitchat about That

Sherri's color palette is a great example of how combining different fabric collections can work so well. Sherri chose sunny yellows for her block centers, and I love how the cool blues and grays frame them.

~ Corey

ASSEMBLING THE QUILT TOP

1. Lay out the blocks in eight rows of eight blocks each. With this block, you don't have to worry about opposing seam allowances. You can just enjoy creating a pleasing arrangement of prints and colors.

2. Sew the blocks together in rows and then sew the rows together. The quilt top should measure 64½" square.

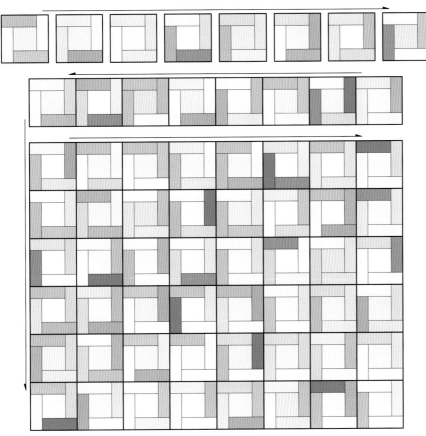

Quilt assembly

FINISHING THE QUILT

For help with any of the finishing steps, go to ShopMartingale.com /HowtoQuilt.

1. Layer the backing, batting, and quilt top. Baste the layers together and quilt as desired. Sherri's quilt is machine quilted with dense allover quilting. The long-arm pattern is a whimsical floral design called Mike's Daisy. It adds a fun touch to this quilt made up of squares and rectangles.

2. Trim the excess batting and backing. Use the 2¼"-wide strips to prepare binding and attach it to the quilt.

REMEMBRANCE

Designed and pieced by **SHERRI McCONNELL**; quilted by **VAL KRUEGER**

This Star quilt is simple to piece and includes just one block that's repeated five times. The secondary patterns that are created, along with the mix of scrappy fabrics, make the design appear much more intricate.

MATERIALS

Yardage is based on 42"-wide fabric.

⅝ yard *total* of assorted red prints for blocks
¼ yard *each* of 5 white tone-on-tone prints
    for blocks
½ yard of red solid for inner border and binding
1 yard of white tone on tone for setting
    triangles and outer border
1¼ yards of fabric for backing
40" × 40" piece of batting

CUTTING

All measurements include ¼"-wide seam allowances.

From the assorted red prints, cut:
40 squares, 2" × 2"
20 squares, 2½" × 2½"
40 rectangles, 2" × 3½"

From *each* white tone-on-tone print, cut:
1 square, 3½" × 3½" (5 total)
4 squares, 2½" × 2½" (20 total)
16 squares, 2" × 2" (80 total)

Continued on page 41

39

Finished quilt: 34" × 34" ◈ Finished block: 9" × 9"

Continued from page 39

From the red solid, cut:

4 strips, 1½" × 42"; crosscut into:
    2 strips, 1½" × 26"
    2 strips, 1½" × 28"*
4 strips, 2¼" × 42"

From the white tone on tone, cut:

1 strip, 14" × 42"; crosscut into:
    1 square, 14" × 14"; cut into quarters
       diagonally to yield 4 triangles
    2 squares, 7¼" × 7¼"; cut in half diagonally
       to yield 4 triangles
4 strips, 3½" × 42"; crosscut into:
    2 strips, 3½" × 28"*
    2 strips, 3½" × 34"*

It's always best to measure the quilt top before cutting border strips to the final length.

Red and White in All Sizes

A few years ago, I made a beautiful scrappy red-and-white sampler quilt. I was inspired by the *Infinite Variety* exhibit of red-and-white quilts at the American Folk Art Museum in New York City. I used the Moda Building Blocks pattern and pieced my scrappy quilt almost entirely from my stash. I use the full-size quilt for trunk shows and lectures. I try to keep it in pristine condition and don't get to enjoy it very much. For several years I've wanted to make a smaller red-and-white quilt to hang in my home; that was the inspiration for this quilt. When I began piecing these blocks, I found a box of scraps from my larger quilt and was able to use many of the same fabrics. Now I can enjoy my red-and-white quilt all the time!

~ Sherri

CONSTRUCTING THE BLOCKS

Press the seam allowances as indicated by the arrows in the illustrations.

1. Draw a diagonal line from corner to corner on the wrong side of the white 2½" squares and place one right sides together with a red print 2½" square. Sew ¼" on each side of the drawn line. Cut on the drawn line and press to make two half-square-triangle units. Trim the units to measure 2" square. Make 40 half-square-triangle units.

Make 40 units.

2. Arrange and sew two red 2" squares and two half-square-triangle units in rows. Join the rows to make a corner unit that measures 3½" square, including seam allowances. Make 20.

Make 20 units,
3½" × 3½".

3. Draw a diagonal line from corner to corner on the wrong side of the white 2" squares and place one right sides together on one end of a red 2" × 3½" rectangle. Sew on the drawn line and press. Trim the seam allowance to ¼". Repeat on the opposite end to make a flying-geese unit that measures 2" × 3½", including seam allowances. Make 40 units.

Make 40 units,
2" × 3½".

4. Sew two flying-geese units together as shown to make a side unit that measures 3½" square, including seam allowances. Make 20 side units.

Make 20 units,
3½" × 3½".

5. Arrange and sew four corner units, four side units, and a white print 3½" square together in three rows. Make sure the flying-geese units and corner units are oriented correctly. Join the rows and press to make a block that measures 9½" square, including seam allowances. Make five blocks.

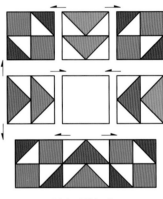

Make 5 blocks,
9½" × 9½".

Two Colors, Lots of Fabrics

I used eight different red fabrics for the flying-geese units, repeating them in each block. I placed the fabrics in the same positions from block to block. That way I could rotate the blocks when setting them together so that the same fabrics didn't end up right next to each other. I also used five different tone-on-tone background fabrics, a different one for each block.

~ Sherri

ASSEMBLING THE QUILT TOP

In steps 3 and 4, press the seam allowances toward the border.

1. Arrange the five blocks, the side setting triangles (cut from the 14" squares), and the corner setting triangles (cut from the 7¼" squares) as shown in the quilt assembly diagram below.

2. Sew the blocks and triangles into diagonal rows and press. Sew the rows together and add the corner setting triangles. The quilt center should measure 26" square, including seam allowances.

Quilt assembly

3. Sew the red solid 1½" × 26" inner-border strips to the sides of the quilt center and press. Sew the red solid 1½" × 28" strips to the top and bottom and press. The quilt center should measure 28" square, including seam allowances.

4. Add the white tone-on-tone 3½" × 28" strips to the sides and press. Add the 3½" × 34" strips to the top and bottom and press. The quilt top should measure 34" square.

Let's Chitchat about That

I've been on a bit of a feather-quilting kick, so when I first saw Sherri's Remembrance quilt, I immediately loved the quilting. It highlights the traditional design beautifully. And I love that touch of whimsy the red polka-dot fabric adds to the quilt.

~ Corey

FINISHING THE QUILT

For help with any of the finishing steps, go to ShopMartingale.com/HowtoQuilt.

1. Layer the backing, batting, and quilt top. Baste the layers together and quilt as desired. Sherri's quilt is machine quilted with curved lines outlining the squares and triangles in the blocks. The side triangles feature a beautiful combination of feathers and curved cross-hatching. The outer border is quilted in a continuous feathered vine.

2. Trim the excess batting and backing. Use the red solid 2¼"-wide strips to prepare binding and attach it to the quilt.

LINEN AND BERRIES

Designed and pieced by **COREY YODER**; quilted by **KAYLENE PARRY**

MATERIALS

Yardage is based on 42"-wide fabric. Fat quarters are 18" × 21". I used a scrappy mix from Moda Fabrics, predominantly fabrics by Fig Tree Quilts and Sherri & Chelsi.

20 red print fat quarters for blocks
20 light print fat quarters for blocks
½ yard *total* of assorted light print scraps
    for blocks
¾ yard of red diagonal stripe for binding
6¾ yards of fabric for backing
81" × 99" piece of batting

When I was first planning my red-and-white quilt, I thought I would use a coral red solid and a white solid. But as I started designing, a new image popped into my head, of scrappy red prints and light prints for the background. Pick all of your favorite low-volume background prints along with your favorite red prints and you'll be on your way to a stunning quilt.

Turn Down the Volume

If you're unfamiliar with the term "low-volume prints," it refers to print fabrics with light backgrounds, which read as light solids. These fabrics tend to have smaller-scale, less-heavy prints. They work very well as background fabrics and add a lot of visual interest to a quilt.

~ *Corey*

Finished quilt: 72½" × 90½" ◆ Finished block: 18" × 18"

CUTTING

All measurements include ¼"-wide seam allowances. Refer to the cutting guides below when cutting the fat quarters.

From *each* light print fat quarter, cut:
2 squares, 7" × 7" (40 total)
10 squares, 3" × 3" (200 total)
16 squares, 2½" × 2½" (320 total)

From *each* red print fat quarter, cut:
2 squares, 7" × 7" (40 total)
10 squares, 3" × 3" (200 total)
5 squares, 2½" × 2½" (100 total)

From the assorted light print scraps, cut:
80 squares, 2½" × 2½"

From the red stripe, cut:
9 strips, 2¼" × 42"

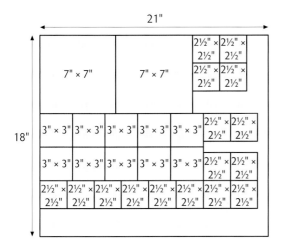

Light fat-quarter cutting guide

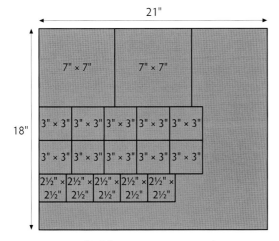

Red fat-quarter cutting guide

CONSTRUCTING THE BLOCKS

Press the seam allowances as indicated by the arrows in the illustrations.

1. Draw a diagonal line from corner to corner on the wrong side of each light print 3" square.

2. Place a marked square right sides together on top of a red print 3" square. Stitch ¼" from each side of the drawn line. Cut along the drawn line to yield two half-square-triangle units. Trim the units to 2½" square. Make 400 half-square-triangle units.

Make 400 units.

3. Choose four half-square-triangle units from the same red print, a matching red print 2½" square, and four assorted light print 2½" squares. Arrange and sew the pieces together in three rows as shown. Sew the rows together to make a Friendship Star block. The block should measure 6½" square, including seam allowances. Make 100 Friendship Star blocks.

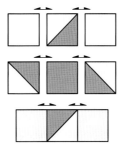 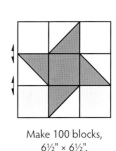

Make 100 blocks,
6½" × 6½".

4. Draw a diagonal line from corner to corner on the wrong side of the light print 7" squares and repeat step 2 using the red print 7" squares

to make 80 large half-square-triangle units. Press and trim the units to 6½" square.

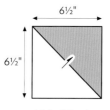

Make 80 units.

5. Arrange and sew five Friendship Star blocks and four 6½" half-square-triangle units in three rows as shown. Sew the rows together to create a block that measures 18½" square, including seam allowances. Make 20 large blocks.

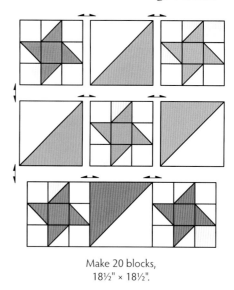

Make 20 blocks,
18½" × 18½".

Let's Chitchat about That

Corey's red-and-white quilt is beautiful! I've always been a fan of the Fig Tree fabrics palette, and this combination of prints in reds and whites is striking. The happy blend of Friendship Stars and half-square triangles lets the lovely fabrics steal the show in this design.

~ *Sherri*

ASSEMBLING THE QUILT TOP

1. Arrange the blocks in five rows of four blocks each. Join the blocks in each row.

2. Join the rows. The quilt top should now measure 72½" × 90½".

This Way or That?

The blocks in this quilt can be rotated in a variety of ways to completely change the look. Play around with the final blocks to see what you come up with!

~ Corey

FINISHING THE QUILT

For help with any of the finishing steps, go to ShopMartingale.com/HowtoQuilt.

1. Layer the backing, batting, and quilt top. Baste the layers together and quilt as desired. Corey's quilt is machine quilted in an allover Baptist clam design.

2. Trim the excess batting and backing. Use the red stripe 2¼"-wide strips to prepare binding and attach it to the quilt.

Quilt assembly

GLADDENING

Designed and pieced by **COREY YODER**; quilted by **KAYLENE PARRY**

MATERIALS

Yardage is based on 42"-wide fabric. This quilt uses Return to Winter's Lane by Kate & Birdie for Moda Fabrics.

2⅓ yards of cream print for block backgrounds
½ yard of taupe print for pinwheels
1 Moda Jelly Roll *or* 40 assorted print strips,
     2½" × 42", for blocks and binding
3½ yards of fabric for backing
63" × 77" piece of batting

Before You Cut

Sort the 2½" strips into two groups of 20 strips each. When dividing the strips, separate them as evenly as possible by color and print. Paying attention to the colors in each group of 20 will guarantee a pleasing distribution of fabrics.

~ Corey

All you need for a quick and festive quilt is an eye-catching Moda Jelly Roll (or some assorted strips), a fabric for the pinwheels, and a background fabric. This quilt is quick to piece, making it fun to sew even during the busy holiday season.

Finished quilt: 56½" × 70½"   ◆   Finished block: 14" × 14"

CUTTING

All measurements include ¼"-wide seam allowances.

From the cream print, cut:
4 strips, 3" × 42"; crosscut into 40 squares,
   3" × 3"
5 strips, 2½" × 42"; crosscut into 80 squares,
   2½" × 2½"
20 strips, 2½" × 42"; crosscut into 160 rectangles,
   2½" × 4½"

From the taupe print, cut:
4 strips, 3" × 42"; crosscut into 40 squares,
   3" × 3"

From *each of 20* assorted print 2½" strips, cut:*
1 rectangle, 2½" × 14½" (20 total)
1 rectangle, 2½" × 10½" (20 total)
1 rectangle, 2½" × 6½" (20 total)
1 square, 2½" × 2½" (20 total)

From *each of 20* assorted print 2½" strips, cut:*
1 rectangle, 2½" × 10½" (20 total)
1 rectangle, 2½" × 6½" (20 total)
1 square, 2½" × 2½" (20 total)

*Save the leftover pieces from cutting the strips
to use for a scrappy binding.*

CONSTRUCTING THE BLOCKS

Press the seam allowances as indicated by the
arrows in the illustrations.

1. Draw a diagonal line from corner to corner
on the wrong side of each cream 3" square.

2. Place a marked cream square right sides
together on top of a taupe 3" square. Stitch ¼"
from each side of the drawn line. Cut along the
drawn line and press to yield two half-square-
triangle units. Trim the units to 2½" square.
Make 80 half-square-triangle units.

Make 80 units.

3. Sew a cream 2½" square to each end of a
print 2½" × 10½" rectangle. Make 40 units that
measure 2½" × 14½".

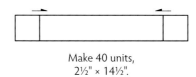

Make 40 units,
2½" × 14½".

4. Sew a cream 2½" × 4½" rectangle to each
end of a print 2½" × 6½" rectangle. Make 40
units that measure 2½" × 14½".

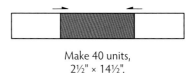

Make 40 units,
2½" × 14½".

5. Sew together two half-square-triangle units,
two cream 2½" × 4½" rectangles, and one print
2½" square. Make sure the half-square-triangle
units are oriented as shown. Make 40 units
that measure 2½" × 14½", including seam
allowances.

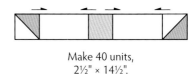

Make 40 units,
2½" × 14½".

6. Sew together a print 2½" × 14½" rectangle
and two of each of the units made in steps 3–5
as shown. Make 20 blocks that measure 14½"
square, including seam allowances.

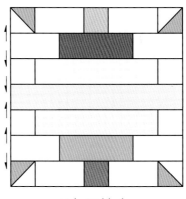

Make 20 blocks,
14½" × 14½".

ASSEMBLING THE QUILT TOP

1. Arrange the blocks in five rows of four blocks each, rotating the blocks as shown in the quilt assembly diagram below. Join the blocks in each row.

2. Join the rows to complete the quilt top. It should measure 56½" × 70½".

Let's Chitchat about That

Corey's Christmas quilt is such a joyful design. Pinwheels always remind me of Christmas, so it was a delight to see the block incorporated into her quilt. I love the mix of fabric prints and colors as well—their placement is just perfect!

~ *Sherri*

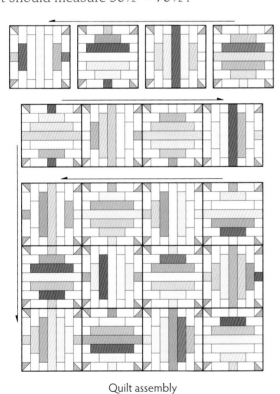

Quilt assembly

FINISHING THE QUILT

For more details on quilting and finishing, go to ShopMartingale.com/HowtoQuilt.

1. Layer the backing, batting, and quilt top. Baste the layers together and quilt as desired. Corey's quilt is machine quilted in an allover feather design.

2. Trim the excess batting and backing. Use the leftover 2½"-wide strips to prepare approximately 266" of binding and attach it to the quilt.

Chitchat about the Design

When I originally wrote the pattern instructions, I planned to have all seam allowances in the final block pressed open. I don't typically press blocks open as I much prefer to "nest" seams within the quilt, pressing them to the side in opposing directions. Figuring out pressing directions is one of my least favorite pattern-writing tasks. Luckily, as I was piecing the quilt top, I realized there was indeed an easy way to press that allowed all the seams to nest nicely. Incidentally, my grandma, who was born in the 1920s, told me that when she began piecing quilts, all seam allowances were pressed open.

The pinwheels in my quilt remind me of little peppermint candies, popular around the holidays. However, by changing out the fabrics to cheerful brights, this design could easily become a summer quilt.

To make an extra-cozy wintertime quilt, opt for plush minky fabric or flannel fabric as the quilt backing. In my household, quilts backed in minky are always the ones in use.

~ Corey

DELIGHT

Designed and pieced by **SHERRI McCONNELL**; quilted by **MARION BOTT**

MATERIALS

Yardage is based on 42"-wide fabric.

1 Moda Jelly Roll *or* 40 strips, 2½" × 42", of assorted red, green, and cream prints for blocks

10 strips, 2½" × 42", of assorted red, green, and cream prints for blocks

⅞ yard of cream tone on tone for setting triangles

1 yard of cream floral for border

⅝ yard of red check for binding

4½ yards of fabric for backing

73" × 82" piece of batting

Use a Moda Jelly Roll, a combination of leftover strips, or 2½" strips cut from your stash to make this easy-to-piece, delightfully happy, scrappy Christmas quilt. Using just one print for the setting triangles will help unify the entire design.

Fabric Notes

I used one Moda Jelly Roll for this quilt and added in several other half-strips (2½" × 21") from my scraps to end up with the number of pieces needed. For a scrappier look, you can use 99 *different* half-strips. Or, if you prefer a more balanced color plan, keep a tally of how many strips of each color you're using. I used 33 strips each of green, red, and cream.

~ *Sherri*

CUTTING

All measurements include ¼"-wide seam allowances.

From the Moda Jelly Roll and 2½" × 42" strips, cut:
99 strips, 2½" × 21"

From the cream tone on tone, cut:
2 strips, 10" × 42"; crosscut into 7 squares, 10" × 10". Cut into quarters diagonally to make 28 triangles (2 are extra).
2 squares, 5½" × 5½"; cut in half diagonally to make 4 triangles

From the cream floral, cut:
7 strips, 4" × 42"

From the red check, cut:
8 strips, 2¼" × 42"

CONSTRUCTING THE BLOCKS

Press the seam allowances as indicated by the arrows in the illustrations.

1. Sew three 2½" × 21" strips together to make a strip set. I used a red, green, and cream strip in each set and placed the cream in the center. Make 33 strip sets that measure 6½" × 21".

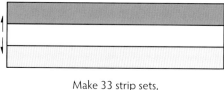

Make 33 strip sets,
6½" × 21".

2. Cut each strip set into three segments, 6½" × 6½", to make the blocks. Make 99 blocks (you will use 98; 1 is extra).

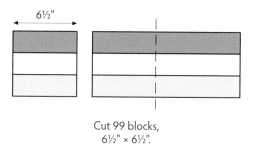

Cut 99 blocks,
6½" × 6½".

Even and Easy Layout

When cutting the blocks from the strip sets, I placed one block from each strip set in a stack to make three stacks. Then I shuffled the blocks in each pile. Finally, I stacked the three piles on top of one another. Then I began laying out the blocks for my quilt top, working in rows one after the other. This ensured an even distribution of most of the prints throughout the quilt.

~ *Sherri*

ASSEMBLING THE QUILT TOP

1. Lay out the blocks on point, rotating them as shown in the quilt assembly diagram below. I kept the reds and greens in the same positions in each row, resulting in a vertical zigzag pattern of reds and greens in the center of the quilt.

2. Sew the blocks into diagonal rows, adding side setting triangles to the left and right ends of the rows. Sew the rows together.

3. Add the corner setting triangles to the corners of the quilt center.

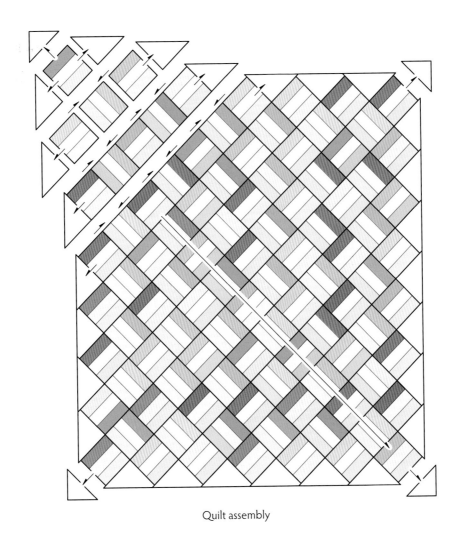

Quilt assembly

Finished quilt: 67" × 75½"   Finished block: 6" × 6"

4. Trim and square up the edges of the quilt, leaving ¼" beyond the points of the blocks.

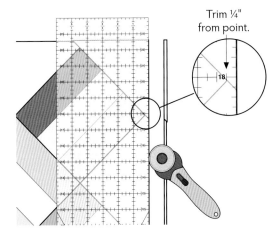

Trim ¼"
from point.

5. Piece the cream floral 4" × 42" strips together to make one long length. Measure the length of the quilt top through the center and cut two strips to that length. Sew these borders to the sides of the quilt.

6. Measure the width of the quilt top through the center, including the borders just added, and cut two strips to that length. Sew these strips to the top and bottom of the quilt. The quilt top should measure approximately 67" × 75½".

Adding borders

FINISHING THE QUILT

For help with any of the finishing steps, go to ShopMartingale.com/HowtoQuilt.

1. Layer the backing, batting, and quilt top. Baste the layers together and quilt as desired. Sherri's quilt is machine quilted in a dense allover pattern called Garden Trellis, a mix of curves and geometric designs that fits well with the Christmas theme.

2. Trim the excess batting and backing. Use the red check 2¼"-wide strips to prepare binding and attach it to the quilt.

PIER 44

Designed and pieced by **SHERRI McCONNELL**; quilted by **MARION BOTT**

MATERIALS

Yardage is based on 42"-wide fabric.

8¼ yards *total* of assorted medium to dark prints for blocks

4⅝ yards *total* of white tone on tones and solids for blocks

⅝ yard of pink print for binding

3½ yards of fabric for backing

63" × 71" piece of batting

Paper for foundation piecing

Fabric glue (optional)

Let's Chitchat about That

This delightful and super-scrappy Pineapple block quilt can be made easily by using a paper foundation rather than cutting odd-shaped pieces and using templates. I worked some of my favorite prints into this quilt—scraps I've collected and saved over the years.

After Sherri and I finished designing our quilts on paper, we shared our ideas to make sure we didn't have any quilts that were too similar. We didn't see each other's finished quilts until the week we turned our manuscript in. Sherri's Pier 44 quilt blew me away when I saw it. You all know my love of a scrappy quilt, and this is the quintessential scrap quilt—so pretty!

~ *Corey*

63

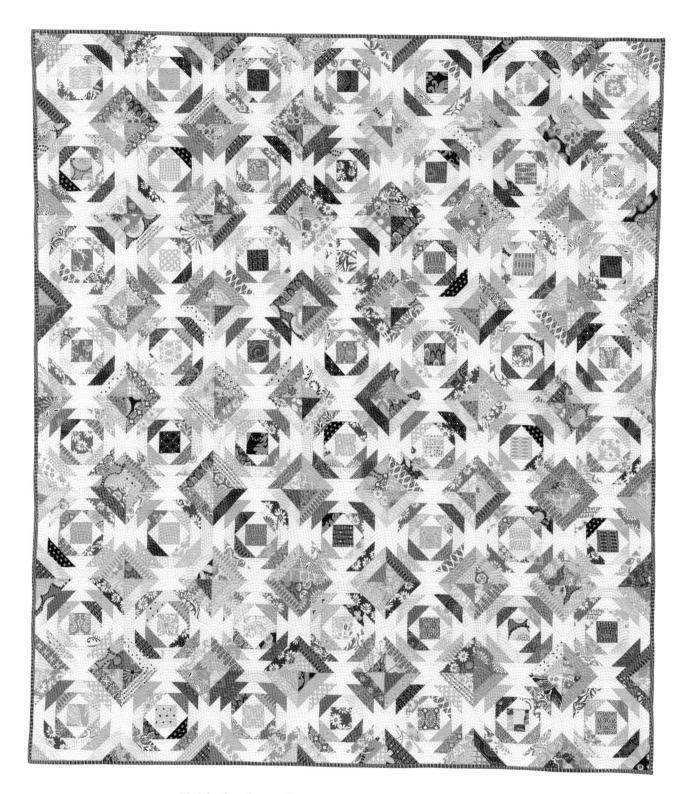

Finished quilt: 56½" × 64½" ◆ Finished block: 8" × 8"

CUTTING

All measurements include ¼"-wide seam allowances.

From the medium and dark prints, cut:
56 squares, 2¾" × 2¾", for piece 1
224 rectangles, 2" × 4", for pieces 6, 7, 8, and 9
224 rectangles, 2" × 5", for pieces 14, 15, 16, and 17
224 rectangles, 2" × 6", for pieces 22, 23, 24, and 25
224 rectangles, 2½" × 4", for pieces 26, 27, 28, and 29

From the whites, cut:
224 rectangles, 2" × 3", for pieces 2, 3, 4, and 5
224 rectangles, 2" × 4", for pieces 10, 11, 12, and 13
224 rectangles, 2" × 5", for pieces 18, 19, 20, and 21

From the pink print, cut:
7 strips, 2¼" × 42"

Another Option

I pieced these blocks using the Creative Grids Pineapple Trim Tool. If you love Pineapple blocks and want to make more quilts or other projects that include this versatile block, you might want to invest in this specialty ruler so you can easily make blocks that finish at 6", 8", or 10" square.

~ *Sherri*

CONSTRUCTING THE BLOCKS

Press the seam allowances as indicated by the arrows in the illustrations.

1. Join the two halves of the foundation pattern on pages 68 and 69. Then make 56 copies of the pattern.

2. Place a print 2¾" square right side up on the unprinted side of the foundation pattern, centering it over the space marked 1. Hold the pattern up to the light to see the outlines from the wrong side. Pin or use a dab of fabric glue to hold the square in place.

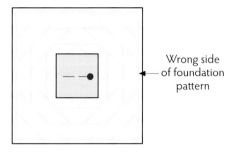

Wrong side of foundation pattern

3. Place a white 2" × 3" rectangle right sides together with the square. Hold it up to the light and make sure it will cover the space marked 2 with enough around the sides for the ¼" seam allowance. Pin the rectangle to the center square.

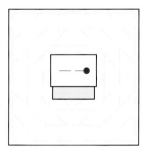

4. Turn the foundation over and sew on the line between pieces 1 and 2, using a short stitch length (12 to 14 stitches per inch). Stitch about ⅛" beyond the lines at the beginning and end.

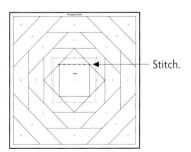

Stitch.

5. Remove the foundation from the machine and turn it over. Fold the white rectangle over to make sure it covers space 2. Fold it back, trim the seam allowance to ¼", and then press. Repeat for spaces 3, 4, and 5.

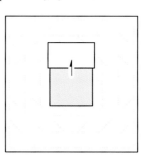

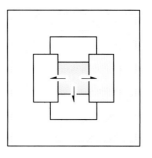

About the Fabrics

The two blocks in the lower-right corner were my inspiration for the entire quilt. I pieced them a few years ago using prints from a variety of Kate Spain collections. I always planned to make an entire quilt with similar blocks, so it felt only right to put them into the quilt in a place where I can easily find them! While I used a lot of Kate Spain fabrics in the rest of the quilt as well, I also included some beautiful bright fabrics by Zen Chic and Crystal Manning, along with favorite prints from my scrap bin. For the background fabrics I used a fun mix of tone-on-tone fabrics by Basic Grey and Zen Chic along with Moda in-house tone on tones and several varieties of solid creamy white fabric.

~ *Sherri*

6. Place a print 2" × 4" rectangle right sides together with pieces 2 and 4 and covering space 6. Pin or glue in place, sew, trim, and press as before. Repeat for spaces 7, 8, and 9.

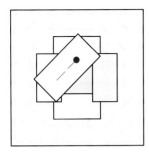

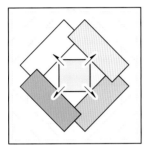

7. Continue adding white and print rounds as indicated on the pattern to complete the block. Press and trim the block to 8½" square, indicated by the dashed lines of the foundation pattern. Leave the paper in place until the blocks are sewn together later. Make 56 blocks.

Make 56 blocks,
8½" × 8½".

ASSEMBLING THE QUILT TOP

1. Arrange the blocks in eight rows of seven blocks each. Sew the blocks together in each row. Remove the paper from the sewn seam allowances and then sew the rows together.

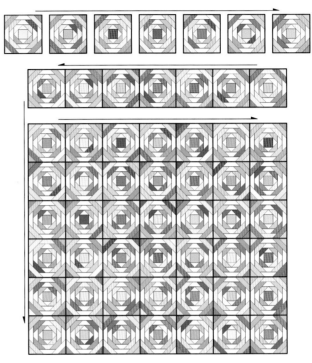

Quilt assembly

2. Carefully remove the remaining foundation papers and press the quilt top. It should measure 56½" × 64½".

FINISHING THE QUILT

For help with any of the finishing steps, go to ShopMartingale.com/HowtoQuilt.

1. Layer the backing, batting, and quilt top. Baste the layers together and quilt as desired. Sherri's quilt is densely machine quilted in an allover pattern called Baptist clams. The curves of the quilting enhance and add movement to the Pineapple blocks.

2. Trim the excess batting and backing. Use the pink 2¼"-wide strips to prepare binding and attach it to the quilt.

Left Pineapple block

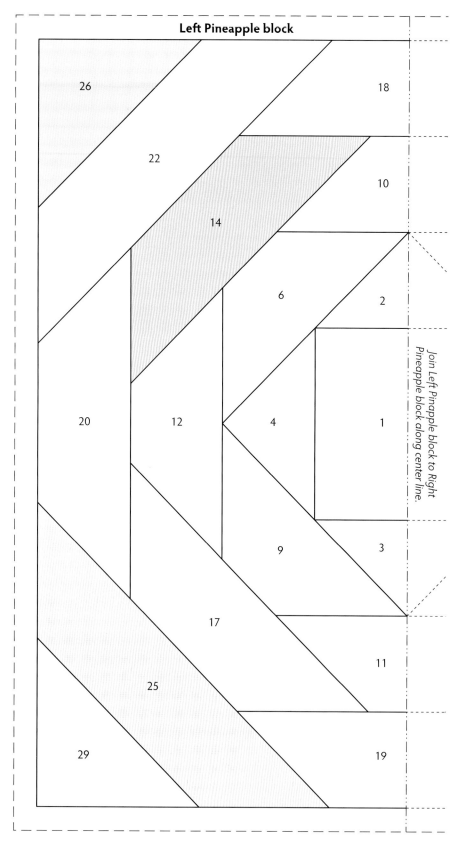

Join Left Pineapple block to Right Pineapple block along center line.

Join and make 56 copies.

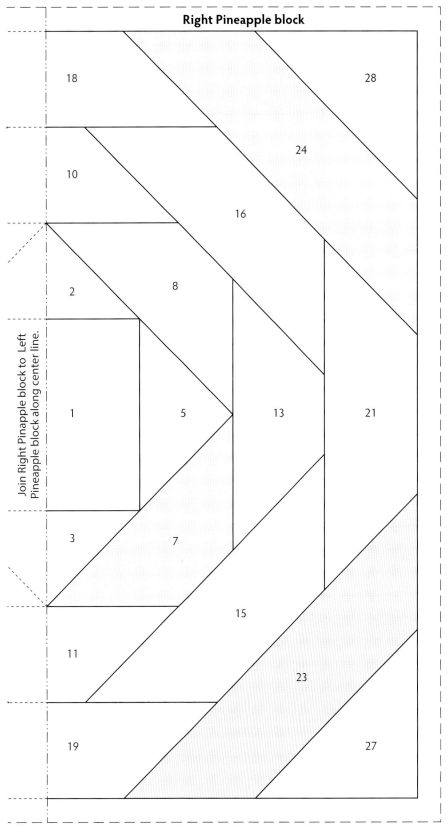

Join Right Pinapple block to Left Pineapple block along center line.

Join and make 56 copies.

DAYFLOWER

Designed and pieced by **COREY YODER**; quilted by **KAYLENE PARRY**

Oh, the Pineapple block! Traditionally, the block is constructed by working out from the center with the triangular "pineapple bits" falling diagonally across the block. I wanted to come up with an easy-to-piece block that mimicked the look of a Pineapple block but that would go together more quickly. This is the result!

MATERIALS

Yardage is based on 42"-wide fabric. I used Nest and Sugar Pie by Lella Boutique for Moda Fabrics.

2 Moda Jelly Rolls *or* 80 assorted print strips, 2½" × 42", for blocks*
2⅞ yards of charcoal textured weave for blocks**
⅝ yard of green stripe for binding
5½ yards of fabric for backing
81" × 99" piece of batting

*See "Length Matters" on page 73. If the strips are not at least 42" long after removing selvages, you may need additional strips.

**Use fabric with some texture, such as Cross Weave from Moda Fabrics.

CUTTING

All measurements include ¼"-wide seam allowances.

From *each of 20* assorted 2½" strips, cut:*
4 rectangles, 2½" × 10½" (80 total)

From *each of 20* assorted 2½" strips, cut:*
2 rectangles, 2½" × 18½" (40 total)
2 squares, 2½" × 2½" (40 total)

*Corey used 10 strips from one Jelly Roll and 10 strips from the second Jelly Roll for a total of 20 strips.

Continued on page 73

Finished quilt: 72½" × 90½"   ◆   Finished block: 18" × 18"

Continued from page 71

From *each of 40* assorted 2½" strips, cut:**
2 rectangles, 2½" × 14½" (80 total)
2 rectangles, 2½" × 6½" (80 total)

From the charcoal fabric, cut:
37 strips, 2½" × 42"; crosscut into 580 squares, 2½" × 2½"

From the green stripe, cut:
9 strips, 2¼" × 42"

***Corey used 20 strips from one Jelly Roll and 20 strips from the second Jelly Roll for a total of 40 strips.*

Let's Chitchat about That

I love, love, love Corey's amazing Pineapple quilt! Corey used a wonderful mix of fabrics, created a simple but striking design layout, and added the gray for a fantastic finish. I love that this quilt is Jelly Roll friendly, too. I'm already thinking of mixing my Clover Hollow and Walkabout collections to make my own version of this one.

~ *Sherri*

Length Matters

The cutting instructions above and on page 71 assume that you can cut a full 42" from each of the 2½" strips. Whether you are using strips cut from yardage or Moda Jelly Roll strips, you should be able to cut the pieces needed. However, if you find you're unable to cut all of the needed pieces from each strip, here are a few suggestions:

◆ Purchase an additional Jelly Roll. This allows you to mix and match three different lines of fabric.

◆ Cut the additional pieces from your stash fabric. This quilt is wonderfully scrappy. Adding coordinating fabrics from your stash will only enhance it.

◆ Purchase an additional 1¼ yards of fabric or the equivalent in smaller cuts. This will give you plenty of fabric for the additional pieces.

~ *Corey*

CONSTRUCTING THE BLOCKS

The instructions are written to make one block at a time. Press the seam allowances as indicated by the arrows in the illustrations.

1. Draw a diagonal line from corner to corner on the wrong side of 28 charcoal 2½" squares.

2. Place a marked square on the left end of a print 2½" × 6½" rectangle, right sides together, orienting the diagonal line as shown. Sew on the marked line. Trim the corner, leaving a ¼" seam allowance, and press. Repeat on the opposite end. The pieced unit will measure 2½" × 6½". Make four units using different prints for each.

Make 4 units,
2½" × 6½".

3. Repeat step 2 with four print 2½" × 10½" rectangles, four print 2½" × 14½" rectangles, and two print 2½" × 18½" rectangles.

Make 4 units,
2½" × 10½".

Make 4 units,
2½" × 14½".

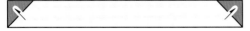

Make 2 units,
2½" × 18½".

4. Sew print 2½" squares to opposite sides of a charcoal 2½" square and press.

Make 1 unit,
2½" × 6½".

5. Sew 2½" × 6½" pieced rectangles to the top and bottom of the unit from step 4, and then sew a 2½" × 6½" pieced rectangle to each side. The block center should measure 6½" × 10½", including seam allowances.

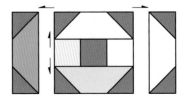

Make 1 block center,
6½" × 10½".

6. Repeat step 5 to add four 2½" × 10½" pieced rectangles to the block center. The unit should measure 10½" × 14½", including seam allowances.

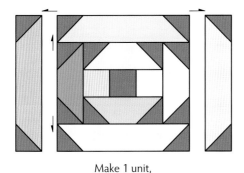

Make 1 unit,
10½" × 14½".

7. Add four 2½" × 14½" pieced rectangles in the same manner to make a unit that measures 14½" × 18½", including seam allowances.

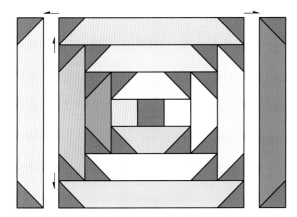

Make 1 unit,
14½" × 18½".

8. Add 2½" × 18½" pieced rectangles to the top and bottom to complete the block, which should measure 18½" square, including seam allowances. Make 20 blocks.

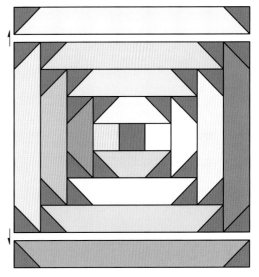

Make 20 blocks,
18½" × 18½".

Chitchat about the Design

I've made a tiny 4" Pineapple block using the Creative Grids Pineapple Trim Tool mini-quilt ruler. This is a great ruler for making 4", 5", and 6" blocks. I love my little 4" block and would enjoy making a whole quilt using these little guys if I could ever carve out enough time. Add that to the bucket list!

When I was working on this block design, I knew I would be a happy camper if my block could use Moda Jelly Roll strips. I had two different Lella Boutique Jelly Rolls that I was itching to mix together. (Notice that sometimes my designs are based on fabrics I want to use?) I was able to tick off all the boxes with this fun design spin on the traditional Pineapple block.

~ *Corey*

Fave Fabrics

I'm frequently asked, "If you weren't sewing with your own fabrics, whose fabrics would you be using?" I do have some favorite designers; for instance, I always love Vanessa Goertzen of Lella Boutique's fabrics. To make my quilt Dayflower, I combined two of her lines to make one great quilt. If you find a designer you like, keep an eye on his or her upcoming lines. Chances are good you'll fall in love with their future lines. Another bonus is that a designer's lines usually mix well with each other. This is perfect if you enjoy making scrappier quilts or if you need to pick up a bit more yardage to complete an in-progress project.

~ Corey

ASSEMBLING THE QUILT TOP

1. Arrange the blocks in five rows of four blocks each, rotating every other block as shown in the quilt assembly diagram below.

2. Join the blocks into rows and press. Join the rows and press. The quilt top should measure 72½" × 90½".

FINISHING THE QUILT

For help with any of the finishing steps, go to ShopMartingale.com/HowtoQuilt.

1. Layer the backing, batting, and quilt top. Baste the layers together and quilt as desired. Corey's quilt is machine quilted with an echoing orange-peel design.

2. Trim the excess batting and backing. Use the green stripe 2¼"-wide strips to prepare binding and attach it to the quilt.

Quilt assembly

Let's Talk Jelly Rolls

Jelly Rolls can add an instant air of scrappiness to any quilt. Below are some tips to help you mix and match *different* Jelly Rolls for an even scrappier look. Plus I have a tip so you can get that ¼" seam allowance just right, despite the pinked edges on those strips.

◆ If you have worked with precut strips, you've probably noticed they can vary slightly in width depending on the manufacturer. I find Moda Jelly Rolls run on the generous side when measured from the "mountain peaks" of the pinked edges, and they're pretty much spot on 2½" when measured from the "valley" of the pinked edge to the opposite valley. Always measure the width of your strips before you begin a project. That way you'll know how to determine your ¼" seam allowance, measuring from the peak or the valley, and whether you need to make any other adjustments.

◆ For a scrappier quilt, choose two different fabric lines for your Moda Jelly Rolls. Feeling less scrappy? Choose two Jelly Rolls from the same fabric line. Alternatively, cutting 2½" strips from your fabric stash in all different fabrics would make an amazing scrappy quilt.

◆ When I'm mixing Jelly Rolls within a quilt, I like to make sure I'll have the fabrics from each set spread throughout the quilt. I like to distribute the colors, prints, and two fabric lines equally. The "Cutting" footnotes on pages 71 and 73 detail how I split up the Jelly Rolls when cutting. As you choose strips, be sure to pay attention to the prints and colors as well. For example, don't use all the large-scale florals in the first cutting step. Evenly distribute them throughout the strip cutting.

◆ As quilters, we've all left the house with bits of thread clinging to our clothes. If you use precuts, including Jelly Rolls, you may notice a bunch of lint added to that mix. Run a lint roller over each side of the Jelly Roll before opening it up. This will eliminate a lot of the extra lint.

◆ Save leftover Jelly Roll strips! They make perfect binding strips for future projects.

~ Corey

RAINWASHED

Designed and pieced by **COREY YODER**; quilted by **KAYLENE PARRY**

MATERIALS

*Yardage is based on 42"-wide fabric. Fat quarters are 18" × 21". I used Sunnyside Up by Corey Yoder for Moda Fabrics.**

3⅓ yards of white solid for blocks and block centers

20 assorted print fat quarters for blocks

⅓ yard of light gray textured weave for block centers

⅝ yard of multicolored diagonal stripe for binding

5 yards of fabric for backing

73" × 89" piece of batting

Rainwashed is a twin-size quilt. For a full-size, you'll need to make 5 more blocks, using 5 more fat quarters, and 4 yards of white solid.

Scrappy brights + lots of white = two favorites! Add a jazzy block to the mix and it's a three-fer. While it's not your typical Courthouse Steps block, the construction is the same. It's also a close relative of the versatile Log Cabin block and equally fun to play with.

Choosing Fabrics

If you'd like the colored prints to stand out, choose a white-background print for the block centers so your eye won't be drawn to the block centers. For more drama and contrast, choose a stronger, darker print for the block centers.

~ *Corey*

Finished quilt: 64½" × 80½" ◆ Finished block: 16" × 16"

CUTTING

All measurements include ¼"-wide seam allowances.

From the white solid, cut:

2 strips, 4½" × 42"; crosscut into 10 squares,
    4½" × 4½"

34 strips, 1½" × 42"; crosscut into:
    20 rectangles, 1½" × 16½"
    20 rectangles, 1½" × 14½"
    20 rectangles, 1½" × 11½"
    20 rectangles, 1½" × 9½"
    20 rectangles, 1½" × 6½"
    20 rectangles, 1½" × 4½"

24 strips, 2" × 42"; crosscut into:
    20 rectangles, 2" × 14½"
    20 rectangles, 2" × 11½"
    20 rectangles, 2" × 9½"
    20 rectangles, 2" × 6½"

From *each* fat quarter, cut:

1 rectangle, 2" × 14½" (20 total)
1 rectangle, 2" × 11½" (20 total)
1 rectangle, 2" × 9½" (20 total)
1 rectangle, 2" × 6½" (20 total)
1 rectangle, 1½" × 16½" (20 total)
1 rectangle, 1½" × 14½" (20 total)
1 rectangle, 1½" × 11½" (20 total)
1 rectangle, 1½" × 9½" (20 total)
1 rectangle, 1½" × 6½" (20 total)
1 rectangle, 1½" × 4½" (20 total)

From the light gray fabric, cut:

2 strips, 4½" × 42"; crosscut into 10 squares,
    4½" × 4½"

From the multicolored stripe, cut:

8 strips, 2¼" × 42"

Check Your Seam Allowance

When piecing the Courthouse Steps blocks, a scant ¼" seam allowance will be your best friend. What is considered a scant ¼" seam? Typically, it's a seam that's a thread or two shy of the full ¼".

~ Corey

CONSTRUCTING THE BLOCKS

Press the seam allowances as indicated by the arrows in the illustrations.

1. Sew white 1½" × 4½" rectangles to the sides of a light gray 4½" square and press. Sew white 1½" × 6½" rectangles to the top and bottom.

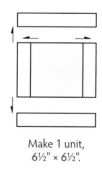

Make 1 unit,
6½" × 6½".

2. Sew assorted print 2" × 6½" rectangles to the sides of the unit and press. Sew print 2" × 9½" rectangles to the top and bottom.

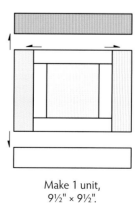

Make 1 unit,
9½" × 9½".

3. Sew white 1½" × 9½" rectangles to the sides of the unit and press. Sew white 1½" × 11½" rectangles to the top and bottom.

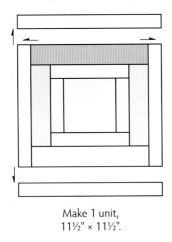

Make 1 unit,
11½" × 11½".

4. Sew print 2" × 11½" rectangles to the sides of the unit and then sew print 2" × 14½" rectangles to the top and bottom.

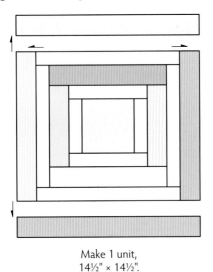

Make 1 unit,
14½" × 14½".

5. Sew white 1½" × 14½" rectangles to the sides of the unit and then sew white 1½" × 16½" rectangles to the top and bottom to complete block A. The block should measure 16½" square, including seam allowances. Make 10 of block A.

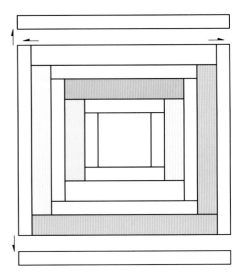

Make 10 of block A,
16½" × 16½".

6. Sew assorted print 1½" × 4½" rectangles to the top and bottom of a white 4½" square and press. Sew print 1½" × 6½" rectangles to the sides.

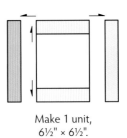

Make 1 unit,
6½" × 6½".

7. Repeat steps 2–5 using white rectangles instead of print, and print rectangles instead of white. After you add the last round of print rectangles, the block should measure 16½" square, including seam allowances. Make 10 of block B.

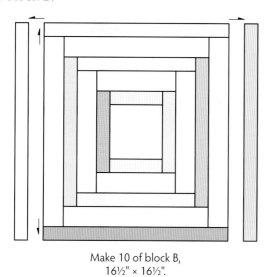

Make 10 of block B,
16½" × 16½".

Chitchat about the Design

As I started designing my quilt, I began with the block as we all know it, with very specific color placement and consistent strip widths. I like the block as it is traditionally done, but I wanted to spice it up a little. The first change I made was to alter the consistent strip width. You'll notice I use both narrow and wide strips in my blocks.

The second change was the addition of a white solid. My first block was made with 100% prints, and I loved what adding white did to the block.

Lastly, I alternated the center squares of my blocks. Some begin with a print in the center, and others begin with white in the center. The blocks are still constructed like a Courthouse Steps block, but the changes completely transform the look of my quilt design.

~ Corey

It's on the List

A quilt made of vintage sheet fabrics is on my bucket list. I would really like to try them with the Rainwashed design. I've been collecting vintage sheets and have a growing stash of them, but that's as far as I've gotten!

~ Corey

ASSEMBLING THE QUILT TOP

1. Arrange the blocks in five rows of four blocks each, alternating block A and block B as shown in the quilt assembly diagram below. Orient block A so that the white 1½" × 16½" rectangles are on the top and bottom of the block. Orient block B so that the print 1½" × 16½" rectangles are on the left and right sides. This way you won't have to match seams from block to block.

2. Join the blocks into rows and then join the rows. The quilt top should measure 56½" × 70½".

Quilt assembly

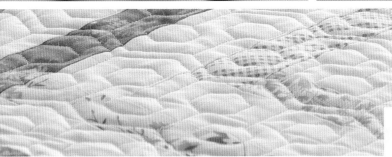

FINISHING THE QUILT

For help with any of the finishing steps, go to ShopMartingale.com/HowtoQuilt.

1. Layer the backing, batting, and quilt top. Baste the layers together and quilt as desired. Corey's quilt is machine quilted in an allover hexagon pattern.

2. Trim the excess batting and backing. Use the multicolored stripe 2¼"-wide strips to prepare binding and attach it to the quilt.

Let's Chitchat about That

Corey's beautiful fabrics and the juxtaposition with the white pieces make Rainwashed a very modern take on the classic Courthouse Steps block. This is definitely going on my must-make list too! You'll notice that where I used smaller pieces and smaller blocks for my Pineapple and Courthouse Steps quilts, Corey used bigger blocks and wider strips. We never talked about this, but I'm delighted that the book includes a larger block and a smaller block option for both of these projects!

~ Sherri

NANTUCKET

Designed and pieced by **SHERRI McCONNELL**; quilted by **VAL KRUEGER**

The classic Courthouse Steps block meets scrappy fabrics from a variety of recent, but timeless collections by Moda designers Laurie Simpson and Polly Minick. Everything about this quilt seems to say time-honored and quintessential.

MATERIALS

Yardage is based on 42"-wide fabric.

⅞ yard *total* of assorted red prints for blocks
1 yard *total* of assorted blue prints for blocks
1 yard *total* of assorted light prints for blocks
½ yard of blue print for binding
2⅔ yards of fabric for backing
47" × 47" piece of batting

CUTTING

All measurements include ¼"-wide seam allowances.

From the assorted red prints, cut:
13 squares, 2½" × 2½"
12 matching pairs of rectangles, 1½" × 4½"
12 matching pairs of rectangles, 1½" × 6½"
12 matching pairs of rectangles, 1½" × 8½"

From the assorted blue prints, cut:
12 squares, 2½" × 2½"
13 matching pairs of rectangles, 1½" × 4½"
13 matching pairs of rectangles, 1½" × 6½"
13 matching pairs of rectangles, 1½" × 8½"

From the assorted light prints, cut:
25 matching pairs of rectangles, 1½" × 2½"
25 matching pairs of rectangles, 1½" × 4½"
25 matching pairs of rectangles, 1½" × 6½"

From the blue print for binding, cut:
5 strips, 2¼" × 42"

87

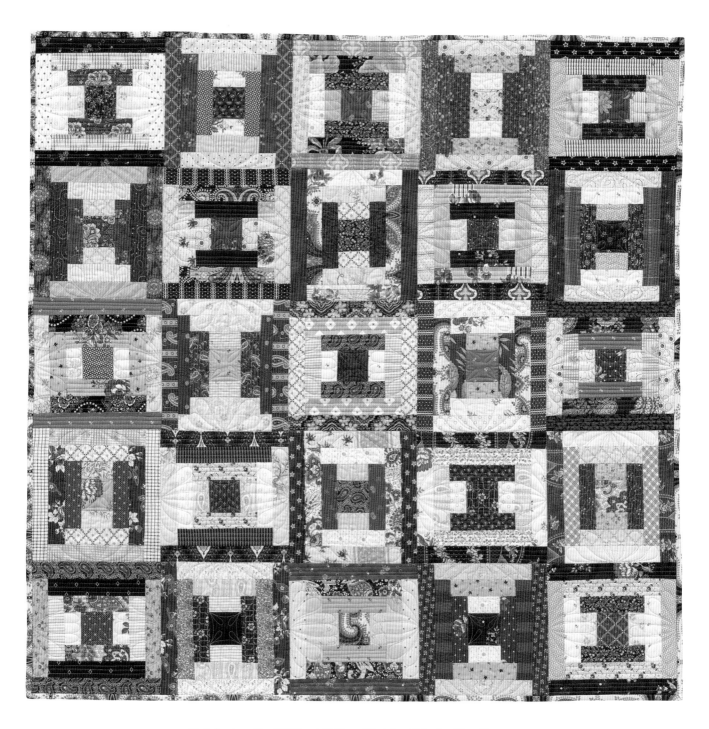

Finished quilt: 40½" × 40½" ◈ Finished block: 8" × 8"

Sort First, Then Sew

Putting all of my cut strips together into piles for each individual block helps me be organized. For this quilt I chose my favorite prints for block centers and then picked the background prints I thought would go best with each center. I also tried to have a bit of contrast in as many blocks as I could between the lights in each block and between the reds or blues. My favorite blocks are the ones that have contrast both between the various light prints and between the various dark prints within each block.

~ Sherri

CONSTRUCTING THE BLOCKS

Press the seam allowances as indicated by the arrows in the illustrations.

1. Sew matching light print 1½" × 2½" rectangles to opposite sides of a red print 2½" square.

Make 1 unit,
2½" × 4½".

2. Sew matching blue 1½" × 4½" rectangles to the top and bottom of the unit.

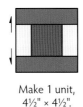

Make 1 unit,
4½" × 4½".

3. Sew matching light 1½" × 4½" rectangles to opposite sides of the unit.

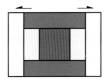

Make 1 unit,
4½" × 6½".

4. Sew matching blue 1½" × 6½" rectangles to the top and bottom of the unit.

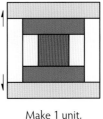

Make 1 unit,
6½" × 6½".

5. Sew matching light 1½" × 6½" rectangles to opposite sides of the unit.

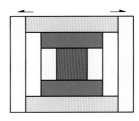

Make 1 unit,
6½" × 8½".

6. Sew matching blue 1½" × 8½" rectangles to the top and bottom of the unit to complete the block. It should measure 8½" square, including seam allowances. Make 13 blocks with red centers.

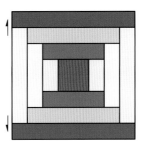

Make 13 blocks,
8½" × 8½".

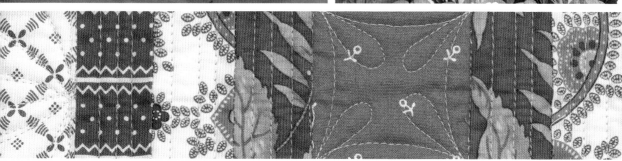

Let's Chitchat about That

Well, add a red-and-blue quilt to my bucket list. It seems that I add a new one to my list every summer. I have some in progress but none finished. As soon as I start seeing red-white-and-blue quilts popping up, especially around Memorial Day and the Fourth of July, the patriotic quilt bug bites me. Sherri's Nantucket quilt has me itching to start working on another quilt . . . or, more realistically, finish the ones I've started.

~ *Corey*

7. Repeat steps 1–6, beginning with a blue 2½" square and adding red rectangles instead of blue. Make 12 blocks with blue centers.

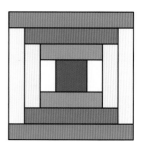

Make 12 blocks,
8½" × 8½".

ASSEMBLING THE QUILT TOP

1. Arrange the blocks in five rows of five blocks each, beginning the top row with a block with a red center. Alternate the blocks with blue and red centers, rotating them as shown in the quilt assembly diagram below. Sew the blocks into rows and press.

2. Sew the rows together and press. The quilt top should measure 40½" square.

FINISHING THE QUILT

For help with any of the finishing steps, go to ShopMartingale.com/HowtoQuilt.

1. Layer the backing, batting, and quilt top. Baste the layers together and quilt as desired. Sherri's quilt is machine quilted with straight lines in the red and blue rectangles and an elegant half-feather design in the light prints. The center squares feature a curved interior outline with a single loop in each corner that echoes the feather shape.

2. Trim the excess batting and backing. Use the blue 2¼"-wide strips to prepare and attach the binding.

A Word about Binding

Our binding instructions call for 2¼"-wide strips, as this is one of the most popular widths for cutting binding. Both of us, however, always cut our binding strips narrower.

Sherri: I usually cut binding strips 2" or 2⅛" wide, depending on the thickness of the batting. This gives a nice, tightly filled binding.

Corey: I prefer to machine bind my quilts. I have found that by cutting the binding 2" wide I can snug it up tight against the edge of the quilt when sewing, and my front and back seams end up a lot tidier. I was never happy with machine binding until I started cutting my strips 2" wide.

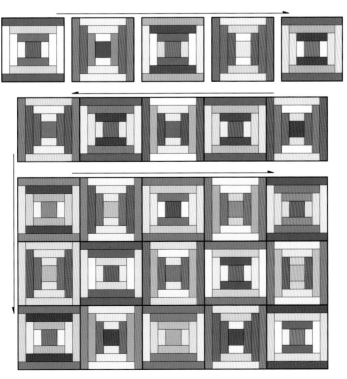

Quilt assembly

Our Favorite Tools

Every quilter has favorite quilting and sewing items. These are the things you must have on hand to begin every project. We've listed a few of our favorites below and explain why we go back to them time after time.

COREY'S FAVORITES

Rulers

I always have these rulers on hand for cutting out quilts.

- 6½" × 18½" Creative Grids
- 6½" square Creative Grids
- 4" × 36" O'Lipfa
- Stripology

I use the 6½" square ruler most often to trim and square up half-square-triangle units. The 36" ruler is wonderful for cutting strips from large pieces of fabric. I have a large 34½" × 46½" cutting mat, so I have plenty of room for this longer ruler. The Stripology ruler is my most recent ruler purchase. I don't know how I ever managed without it! It has become invaluable in the amount of time it saves me. It allows me to cut multiple strips of fabric without moving the ruler. It features numerous vertical "slits" that rotary cutters fit into across the entire ruler. Depending on strip size, I can cut hundreds of pieces without moving the ruler.

Thread

Aurifil 50-weight white thread is my favorite for piecing. This finer thread will lead to more accurate piecing and also less bobbin filling. I never gave a lot of thought to thread when I began making quilts almost 20 years ago. But I soon realized that the right thread makes a big difference.

Notions

There aren't a lot of sewing notions that I must have, but there are two I wouldn't be without.

The Clover Thread Cutter Pendant is basically a small, roughly quarter-sized circular cutter disguised as a pendant. It has little notches cut around the whole perimeter where threads can be cut. It can be worn as a pendant if attached to a chain (which I don't do). I keep one beside my sewing machine and one on my ironing board and use them to cut threads when I'm chain piecing. It's faster than snipping with scissors and there's no danger of accidentally snipping into your piecing.

Clearly Perfect Angles is attached to my sewing machine almost 100% of the time. It is a thin plastic guide that clings to the bed of the sewing machine and eliminates the need for drawing diagonal lines when making half-square triangles, flying geese, or stitch-and-flip corners. I am never without this handy tool!

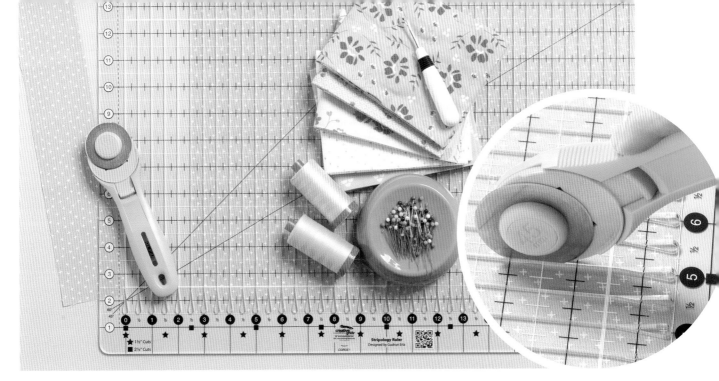

We both love the Stripology ruler—almost as much as we love pretty fabrics!

SHERRI'S FAVORITES

Rulers

These are the rulers I can't live without.

- 8½" × 24½" Creative Grids
- 6½" × 12" Creative Grids or 8½" × 12" Omnigrid
- 4½" × 8½" Creative Grids
- Stripology—accurately cuts strips in record time!
- Bloc Loc Flying Geese
- 6½" square Fit to Be Quarter

I use the 24½" ruler when cutting from yardage. When cutting smaller pieces of fabric, I like to use a smaller ruler such as the 12"-long ruler, which I've used for years. I recently got the 4½" × 8½" ruler, which I love as well! Like Corey, I love the Stripology ruler. It saves an incredible amount of time cutting strips and then being able to crosscut them quickly into dozens and dozens of squares. The Bloc Loc Flying Geese rulers are my absolute favorite ruler for making flying geese! And I love the Fit to Be Quarter 6½" square by Monique Dillard of Open Gate Quilts for squaring up half-square triangles and quarter-square triangles.

Thread

Aurifil thread works well in my machine and comes in gorgeous colors. It's also very durable and works well for machine piecing and binding!

Notions

For me, the following items make a big difference.

The Clover seam ripper is the love of my sewing life! I always have it nearby.

Small design boards, which I make from foam core cut into squares, are very handy. I cover them with batting on one side and finish with binding. I adore these for laying out block pieces.

A pincushion is a necessity. I try to make a new one with each fabric collection.

The Olfa Splash rotary cutter and Olfa Endurance blades are hands-down winners for cutting.

Sherri L. McConnell

I was not going to be a quilter—my grandmother was a quilter, and she cut up perfectly good fabrics just to sew them back together. She went to guild meetings and met with her smaller quilting groups to sew and exchange blocks. She wore quilt block T-shirts and went to quilt shows; she even entered quilt shows and won blue ribbons. My grandmother loved hand quilting in the evenings with her stand-up frame and her lap frame. She made quilts and wall hangings and place mats and table runners. And she gifted many lovely things to me and her other family members.

Because of her, and with her help, I made my very first quilt. Oh, how wise she was! I became a quilter almost overnight. I started making small hand-quilted projects to give to family and friends. I bought quilt books and pored over the lovely pages for inspiration. Slowly, over the years, I found more and more time to sew. I also discovered the wide world of quilting blogs, with inspiration at my fingertips. I bought fabric. I made quilts of all sizes. I started buying quilting T-shirts. I sewed late into the evenings when my children were asleep and my husband was at work. And I met the most wonderful and amazing people who love quilting as much as I do, as my grandmother did, and her grandmothers before her.

I am a quilter! I'm ever-thankful for the love of my family members who have always encouraged and supported me in every aspect of life, including quilting. And I'm also ever-thankful for the quilting community that I know online and in real life. Your encouragement and support and inspiration mean the world to me. Happy quilting!

To keep up with my quilting journey, visit my blog at AQuiltingLife.com.

Corey Yoder

I grew up in and still reside in a small Amish community in Ohio. I come from a line of quilters on both sides of my family and have been surrounded by quilts and fabric my entire life. Quilts were always in the frame waiting to be hand quilted. Quilting get-togethers always meant much laughter and good food.

After I married my husband, Ryan, in 1997 at the age of 19, my love of fabric blossomed. I hadn't sewn while living at home but dived into buying fabric without knowing what I would do with it. It seemed natural to make a quilt, and one quilt quickly led to two and has now turned into hundreds.

I began designing quilts in 2010, and my work has since been featured in many quilting magazines and books. My first book, *Playful Petals,* was published in 2014. I began designing fabric for Moda Fabrics the following year and launched my quilt-pattern business, Coriander Quilts.

The comment I hear most about my fabric designs is, "Your fabrics make me feel happy." I wholeheartedly embrace the idea that quilts and fabric should always bring joy and spread love. For more on my fabrics and patterns, visit CorianderQuilts.com.

Share YOUR *Sunday Best Quilts*

Sherri and Corey love being a part of the lively online quilting community—join them by sharing what you've created from their book!

1 **FOLLOW** them on Instagram—Sherri at **@aquiltinglife**, Corey at **@corianderquilts**.

2 **MAKE** a project from *Sunday Best Quilts* and snap some pics along the way. You can take photos of your fabric selections, sewn units and blocks, quilt tops, and finished quilts. Sherri and Corey would love to see your progress!

3 **SHARE** your photos on Instagram using the hashtag **#SundayBestQuilts**.

Follow Sherri's and Corey's blogs for more quilting fun, including quilt-alongs, videos, tutorials, project reveals, giveaways, and more!

AQuiltingLife.com

CorianderQuilts.com